Funny Gag Gifts and Journals

This journal belongs to:

___

Made in United States
North Haven, CT
02 May 2022

18820021R00078